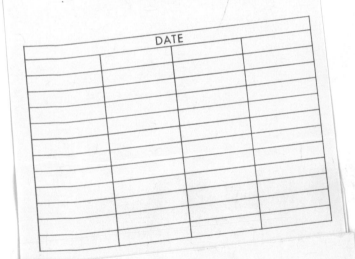

DATE			

*Young Women
in the
World of
Race Horses*

Young Women in the World of Race Horses

Larry Adler

DAVID McKAY COMPANY, INC.

New York

Copyright © 1978 by Larry Adler

Library of Congress Cataloging in Publication Data

Adler, Larry, 1939-
   Young women in the world of race horses.

   SUMMARY: Describes the training and qualifications
necessary for the wide variety of positions open to women
at race tracks and horse farms. Also discusses well-
known female jockeys, trainers, and other women who work
with race horses.
   1. Horse-racing—Vocational guidance—Juvenile literature. 2. Women in horse racing—Juvenile literature.
[1. Horse racing—Vocational guidance— 2. Women in
horse racing. 3. Vocational guidance] I. Title.
SF336.5A34   798'.4'0023   77-20065
ISBN 0-679-20438-5

10 9 8 7 6 5 4 3 2 1

Manufactured in the United States of America

To my father, Duffy

Contents

1

The Dream Job

Early in the morning, often well before sunrise, thousands of young women and girls around the country are wide awake, and ready and eager to start their jobs. They know what is in store for them: a long day, hard physical labor, and a number of outdoor chores that must be done no matter what the weather.

The young women have no employment security. They must be on the job seven days a week, and they will never get rich on their salaries. But they would not trade their jobs for anything else in the world. They're working with thoroughbred horses. And they love it.

Young women who work with thoroughbreds are truly performing a labor of love. Their interest in horses is great and their desire to be near the animals is strong. So they put up with all kinds of discomforts just so they can get what they want: a job that puts them in nose-to-muzzle contact with their handsome four-footed friends.

Employers do not give any special privileges to young women, whose muscles often ache from exertion. The horses do not extend any courtesies to the ladies, either. The animals, each weighing half a ton or more, will just as soon

After a groom separates the clean stable straw from the used, she tosses the old straw into a pit. (The Meadowlands)

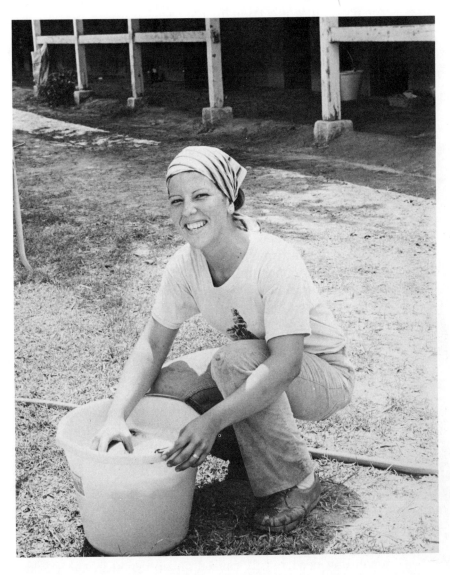

Patty Turner, a groom with the Vernon Andrews stable at Hialeah Park, Hialeah, Fla., is a girl who is happy in her work. (Hialeah Park)

step on a woman's foot as a man's. Thoroughbreds also bite and occasionally kick, so anyone who works with them faces the possibility of getting hurt.

There are two main places where young women are hired to deal with thoroughbreds. One is at race tracks, where the animals are boarded and run. The other is at thoroughbred farms, where horses are bred, raised, trained, rested, and put out to pasture after retirement. Some farms focus solely on breeding and raising foals to sell as yearlings.

Employers at both tracks and farms now realize how expert women are with thoroughbreds. But it wasn't always that way. Until the 1950s women employees on race tracks and horse farms were almost unheard of, although there were a few female trainers. The only women who regularly appeared at tracks and farms were those who owned horses.

By the 1960s new laws and a changing attitude helped create a breakthrough for women looking for additional employment opportunities. Government legislation and women's liberation groups forced job barriers to fall. Women began seeking different outlets for their talents and abilities, and entered fields where they had never before been employed.

The horse racing fraternity became increasingly aware of what was happening in other businesses and industries. However, the people who did the hiring—owners, trainers, and stable foremen—were reluctant to follow the trend. They were, for the most part, a conservative group with an aversion to change. The idea of hiring women was too different, too far out, for them to accept.

But it was impossible to stop progress. Just as an experiment, a few forward-minded employers hired some young women. The women were exceptionally good workers, so more were hired.

Word got around, and soon a major but peaceful worker revolution occurred. It caused an upheaval in the world of thoroughbred racing. It allowed women to take jobs at tracks and farms, jobs that for hundreds of years before had been held exclusively by men.

At first, racing people hired women for purely economic reasons. Employers were not trying to aid the cause of women's liberation, they were trying to help themselves. There was a shortage of willing and able men, and a new labor supply and source of help was needed. In this case, the new source was women.

Although there were, and are, a number of skilled and responsible male hired hands working with thoroughbreds, many were not performing a labor of love—many didn't even like horses, and it showed in the detached, uninvolved way they did their chores. The men lacked a certain quality that comes naturally to a woman and makes her more devoted to the animals she has to care for. In fact, some male workers were coldhearted and short-tempered, and they savagely kicked and beat the horses they were supposed to be looking after.

Men had other shortcomings as well. Some were little more than drifters who applied for the work because it offered them a free place to sleep. Others were alcoholics, and some were downright lazy or not too intelligent. Wages were so low that when several states increased their welfare payments, some of the men managed to get on the relief rolls with virtually no loss of income.

It was no wonder that employers started hiring so many young women. They had perfect qualifications. They got their jobs by choice, not by chance. They were almost always reliable and always sober. They tried harder. They did more for their horses. They were kinder to them. And for the most part, the women were smarter and better educated than the men.

"The biggest things she has going for her are patience and a genuine fondness for horses most men just don't have," said a trainer who had hired one young woman and then added more to his staff.

Another trainer added, "Our horses seem to respond better to girls than men. I don't know why, but the horses seem to sense the love the girls have for them. A horse often can tell the difference between a woman and a man by smell and

Claire Stahlnaker exercises horses for the A. J. Bardaro stable at Hialeah. (Hialeah Park)

voice. We noticed an improvement in the disposition of many of our horses when they were being groomed by a girl rather than a man. Many horses we consider skittish and hard to manage become docile when they are being attended to by a girl. They sense their gentleness and the young women respond accordingly."

By the time the 1970s rolled in, women were accepted by almost all employers. More and more young women were hired, praised, and promoted for the work they did.

It is now easier than ever for a girl to get a job working with thoroughbreds. Opportunities are everywhere. There are tracks as far east as Marshfield Fair in Duxbury, Massachusetts, and as far west as Ferndale, California. There are farms that range as far north as the Circle D, in Scobey, Montana, and as far south as the Roseland Farm in Hollywood, Florida.

In fact, a young woman who wants to work in the sport of thoroughbred racing has a much better chance of having her dream come true than a boy who wants to participate in another sport. There are approximately 1,250 professionals in the National Football League; there are no more than 650 major-league baseball players, and there are only about 260 players in the National Basketball Association. But there are thousands of women in thoroughbred racing. Each year more than 61,000 horses run on tracks, and an additional 28,000 new foals are born. They all need workers to care for them. With so many horses, and so many available jobs, predictions are that the number of female employees will continue to rise.

Employers are so open to hiring women that all any girl needs to land her first job is some elementary knowledge of horses, enough nerve to go knocking on stable doors, and a bit of luck. Girls who want summer work should have as little difficulty obtaining employment as those looking for year-round positions. Most tracks are open only part of the year, and farms also hire seasonal help.

Gaining entrance to a farm is usually easy, although it is

Cindy Long at the Robert Connor stable at Hialeah. (Hialeah Park)

helpful to write a letter beforehand explaining the purpose of the visit. Getting into a track may be harder. Tracks vary a great deal in size and security measures. At some of the smaller courses, where security is looser, a young woman can flash a big smile at the guard at the gate and walk right past him to get to the stables. At other places guards stop young women and issue passes. In certain instances, guards will not allow them through the entrance. They have them fill out application forms or they make an announcement over the loudspeaker and ask if anyone is interested in hiring a beginner.

But anyone who gets a job at a track, beware. To quote one young lady, "Once you've worked on a race track you can never quit. Men get addicted to gambling, but women fall in love forever with the horses."

2

The Work

The ultimate test of any horse is at the track. This is where the crowds cheer and the big money is won.

Some girls like to be near the action and excitement. They start out working at a track on what is called "the backstretch," the name for the behind-the-scenes activities at a race course.

Every backstretch worker's first position is as a "hot walker." It is the easiest and least demanding job there is, and it requires no experience. All that is necessary is an ability to get along with animals.

Trainers and stable foremen or women who are looking for a hot walker will hire and test any girl who seems responsible. If she does her job well, the girl has a future with thoroughbreds.

A hot walker's job begins about 6:00 A.M. She walks on a path around the stable, leading any horse who is not going to be exercised that morning. A horse may not be exercised because it is sore or sick or has been in a race recently, or simply because the trainer wants to give it a day off. The hot walker spends about thirty to forty-five minutes with each animal. By the time the hot walker is finished with these

Trainer N. J. Winick thinks girls are great workers. Among his grooms are, left to right: Dee Marcantel, Sandy Blount, and Jamie Johnson. (Hialeah Park)

thoroughbreds, the first horse to have been exercised on the track has returned to the stable. The hard-run horse is hot and sweaty, and it is winded. It gets a quick sponge bath while the hot walker holds it, and then has a blanket thrown over its back. After that, the hot walker walks the horse, making sure to give it a little water from a hanging bucket every round or so. The hot walker follows the same routine with other horses returning from their workouts.

"Walking hots" is a necessity. If a horse went straight back to its stall after a run, its muscles would tighten up and its chances of catching cold would be greatly increased.

Hot walkers handle a maximum of six horses a day. When the last one is brought back to its stall, a hot walker does one final assignment. She rakes the stable area. Her job is completed before lunchtime, unless one of her horses is running that afternoon. Then she must be available to walk the thoroughbred again when the race is over.

A hot walker may graduate to one of three positions—a groom, an exercise girl, or a pony girl if she is a skilled rider.

A good groom must be honest and give full reports about her charges to her boss. She must be a responsible nursemaid to her horses. She is one of the first to start work in the morning and one of the last to leave in the late afternoon. A groom has a long list of daily assignments: empty the overnight bucket, dump the food bucket, scrub and refill both, remove leg bandages, wipe dust from the horse's coat, comb the mane and tail, remove mud and muck from the horse's hooves, separate clean straw from dirty straw, haul the dirty straw to the muck pit, rake the stall and sprinkle the floor with lime, lay out fresh straw, bridle and saddle the horse for its morning run, check the horse's legs after the workout and rub them with liniment, apply needed medication, bandage the legs, clean the "tack" (the name for all the equipment a horse wears), and give the horse its final afternoon feeding, brushing, and checkover.

Because there is so much to do, a groom can only cope with three or four horses a day.

A good groom is vital to the health and well-being of the horses assigned to her. She knows her thoroughbreds' personalities, and she looks for any changes in their behavior or eating habits, often a sign of sickness. She is fanatical about keeping her horses' hooves clean. Horses sometimes stand in straw that they've fouled with urine and manure, and if their feet aren't cleaned of disease-causing bacteria, an unhealthy condition called "thrush" develops. A good groom knows how to tie bandages with just the right amount of pressure. Leg bandages that are too tight may damage tendons and cripple a horse. A groom who moves up the ladder generally becomes a forewoman or trainer, but a responsible and experienced groom can be an indispensable part of a racing stable, and is regarded as an assistant trainer.

An exercise girl rides thoroughbreds during their workouts. An easy workout is called a "gallop"; a faster one is called a "breeze." An exercise rider needs strong muscles to keep the thoroughbreds under tight control. One girl, who didn't realize this, remembers the first time she tried to exercise a horse. It ran off with her and raced around and around the track for three miles. The embarrassed girl was so tired she almost fell from her saddle before the horse was finally caught.

If an exercise girl begins at the track, she must start out with the quieter horses. But it is easier to learn how to gallop or breeze at a farm, where the animals are younger and have less strength.

An exercise girl gets instructions from the horse's trainer on how fast to ride the thoroughbred over a set distance during its workout. If the girl is good, she will be such an accurate judge of time that she will come within a fraction of a second of carrying out orders. An exercise girl with this ability is said to have "a clock in her head."

An exercise girl makes about the same weekly salary as a groom. Exercisers who have ambition and determination and weigh about 112 pounds or less can become jockeys.

A pony girl leads a thoroughbred by holding its reins while

Patty Turner rakes the front of her trainer's stable area while a watchful thoroughbred looks on. (Hialeah Park)

riding a "lead pony," a horse which may be of any breed. In the morning, a pony girl exercises horses that should not carry the extra weight of a rider because of leg problems or other reasons. In the afternoon, she leads thoroughbreds to the track and keeps the high-strung animals from running off and wearing themselves out before the start of a race.

Pony girls have two advantages over exercise girls. First, the horses pony girls ride are less temperamental and easier to handle than thoroughbreds. Second, pony girls don't have to worry about their weight as much as exercise girls. However, pony girls don't usually become jockeys, because they're often too heavy or not skilled enough to manage a race horse. The amount of money a pony girl makes depends on the number of thoroughbreds she "ponies" during the week.

A stable forewoman works for trainers who have many horses under their care. Her job is to manage the work done by others in the barns. She takes her orders from the trainer, then sees that they are carried out. She makes sure her horses get their required amount of feed, water, vitamins, and medication, and she also checks their health. At some tracks, the forewoman hires personnel.

The trainer has the highest position of anyone working with thoroughbreds at a race track. She is ultimately responsible for the animals under her care. She can work for one stable, for several different owners, or for herself, if she owns her own stock.

The most important part of the trainer's job is to prepare and condition horses so they are in top physical shape for their races. But there is more to a trainer's work than that. The trainer makes purchases, pays bills and salaries, obtains stall space at a track for her horses, and enters them in races. If there is no forewoman, she oversees the stable work as well. If the trainer has a large number of thoroughbreds, help is provided by an assistant trainer.

According to one woman trainer, "The job is like living on Heartbreak Hill." The legs of race horses are extremely fragile, and injuries and disappointments happen more often than victories. But in spite of all her complaints, the trainer comes back every day for more. In her heart, she loves what she is doing.

Trainers generally work for a salary plus a percentage of their horses' winnings, which they collect from the owners. Trainers, in turn, share part of this money with employees who work with the horses. This offers everyone the best possible incentive to do her best.

A trainer puts in months or years of work developing a horse. But when the horse wins an important race, the trainer shares the glory with the jockey.

A prospective girl jockey needs strength, courage, and a will to succeed. She must also be a good athlete. The amount of money she makes depends on how many races she wins. She must know her horse's quirks and traits and handle the animal accordingly. (Two thoroughbreds will respond differently to the same method of treatment.) A good woman jockey, like a good exercise girl, has a clock in her head. She is a master at judging the pace of a race and speeding up or slowing down the speed of her mount. Since a jockey communicates these instructions through the reins, she must have what racing people call "good hands" to make her horse understand and obey her signals.

A jockey gets instructions from the trainer on the strategy to use in each race. Yet once the horses leave the starting gate, she must have enough self-confidence to switch tactics and plans if she thinks that will help her win.

A jockey must have extremely quick reflexes and react without fear. If a space opens up between two blockading thoroughbreds, the rider must instantly respond and rush her horse through. This is one of the riskiest moves in racing. The other two horses may not be as far apart as the jockey thought, or they may unintentionally move back in toward each other. In either case, an accident often happens.

Being a jockey is not for the fainthearted. Girl jockeys have been injured, paralyzed, and even killed. However, the

A hard-working groom can sit for a while when she is cleaning tack, the riding equipment for a horse. (The Meadowlands)

rewards for the work can be high. Jockeys traditionally get ten percent of their horses' winnings. The best female jockeys have won $300,000 and more in a year. (Robyn Smith holds the record for women riders, having won $634,055 in 1973.)

Working at the track as a jockey or backstretch employee has its benefits, yet there are several appealing advantages to working on a thoroughbred farm. On a farm, a girl may get free room and board. A farm worker also stays in one place and does not have to move around the country, packing and unpacking her bags as she follows her horses to different tracks. Most important of all, a girl may find it easier to learn about thoroughbreds on a farm. The pace is more relaxed, the pressure is less intense, and experienced people have more time to pass on their knowledge to newcomers.

At all except the largest farms, workers are general hands and do not have specialized job duties. Each employee will walk, groom, and exercise horses, as well as put up fences, paint, and do any other chores that come her way.

The trainer is the only specialist at a farm. Her job is to prepare young horses for their first race.

Most horses are foaled at the start of the year and taken away from their dams before their first birthday. Then, slowly and carefully, the trainer takes the nervous yearlings and gets them used to such unfamiliar conditions as being bridled, having a bit in their mouths, and being mounted and ridden. After that, the trainer teaches the growing animals how to enter and break from a starting gate and how to run under racing conditions.

A trainer on a farm must be patient yet firm with a young horse, which must not be allowed to fall into bad habits that will invariably cause trouble when it starts racing as a two-year-old.

Besides the positions already described, there are a number of other jobs open to girls who want to work with thoroughbreds. These range from veterinarian to blacksmith to track publicity director.

3

Horses and History

The first organized sporting event held in America was a horse race. It was run in 1665 on a course near the site of the present Belmont Park on Long Island, New York. Horse racing spread throughout the colonies and grew in popularity. It even attracted George Washington, who helped officiate at a race held in South Carolina.

In those early times, American women were forbidden to have anything to do with horse racing except watch it. But in England, men were more lenient. The first women-only horse race was held in Britain in 1723, according to the skimpy records available. The winner was awarded a silver teacup.

Britain was also the site of the first two important races between a man and a woman. Alicia Meynell, the friend of a well-known sportsman, a Colonel Thornton, participated in both races. The first man–versus–woman contest was held in August, 1804, and run over a distance of four miles. It attracted a tremendous crowd of curiosity-seekers and well-wishers.

The twenty-two-year-old Alicia was dressed for the occasion in a leopard-print, full-length dress with blue sleeves, a buff vest, and blue cape. But she wasn't there to win a fashion contest. She was there to win a race, and she was extremely serious about it. A bet of £1,575, a huge sum in those days, had been made between Colonel Thornton and the opposing male jockey. A lot more money had been wagered by others. Alicia did not want to disappoint Thornton or her followers.

As the race was about to start, the horsewoman's opponent purposely bumped into her and then took off. Nevertheless, Alicia caught up with her rival and was the front runner for three long miles. Then her horse tired. She lost the lead and began using her whip. When her worn-out mount was unable to respond, she saw the situation was hopeless and stopped rather than risk injury to the exhausted animal.

Thornton was a poor loser, especially after what the other jockey had done to Alicia at the start. He refused to pay up.

In the following year, 1805, another male jockey accepted a challenge from Alicia Meynell. Again the woman rider took the lead at the start, and again, as the horses galloped toward the finish, she was passed. But only for a moment. Alicia soon retook first place and, after a head-to-head duel down the stretch, won by inches.

"There is something so bold and original in the idea of a lady publicly contending with a man, I think it cannot fail to take prodigiously among all females of rank and spirit," a magazine correspondent wrote after the triumph. Apparently few others shared the reporter's enthusiasm, including Alicia. Content with her one victory, she never rode for money again.

It was approximately a century before another horsewoman made headlines. This time it was in America.

Eleonora Sears, born in 1881, was the great-great-granddaughter of Thomas Jefferson. She came from a rich and socially prominent Boston family. When she was a young girl, people were very prim and proper. Women wore extremely long skirts to hide their legs and ankles. Even the

Soon after Eleonora Sears posed for this photo in 1909, she switched from a long skirt to pants. She created a scandal when she rode astride instead of sidesaddle. (Bettmann Archive)

legs of chairs were sometimes covered. Girls who had what was then considered a correct upbringing rode horses side-saddle and were clothed in outfits that reached not only to the bottoms of their shoes but also up to the tops of their necks.

Eleonora Sears scandalized her family, her social peers, and all of American society by wearing pants and riding a horse astride instead of sidesaddle. Today no one is outraged when girls ride wearing blue jeans, but in Eleonora's time, her costume created a sensation. Editorials were published and sermons preached about the "wicked" lady. But Eleonora just laughed at her critics.

She was adventurous and athletic, one of the first women to drive a car and fly in a plane. She sailed yachts, was a crack shot with both a pistol and rifle, and was the best woman squash player in the country. But more than anything, she loved horses. She played polo, handled steeple-chase horses (horses that jump over hedges and barriers as they race around a track), and ran a full-scale racing stable in Massachusetts.

Because of her accomplishments, including introducing women to riding astride, Eleonora Sears helped pave the way for every horsewoman that came after her.

In 1923 there were outcries against another woman rider, Judy Johnson. Judy started galloping horses at Belmont Park for her father, a trainer, and became, in all probability, the first exercise girl to ever work at a major race track. Judy was booed and yelled at by riders and stablehands, who complained she was taking money out of their pockets. But every day Judy closed her ears and did what made her happy. Like Eleonora Sears, she didn't care what other people said.

Another first was recorded on July 7, 1934, when Mary Hirsch became the first woman to get a trainer's license from a state racing commission. Mary had the same advantage Judy did. Her father was also a trainer, and she had been learning from him ever since she graduated from high school. Less than a year after Mary got her license, Judy did, too.

During World War II, Judy achieved another milestone. She became the first woman to become a licensed steeple-chase rider and compete against men in those races.

There were protesters, of course, but no one paid much attention to them. Steeplechasing was a minor sport. In comparison to thoroughbred racing, the prizes were smaller, the races fewer, and the competition not as brutal. The sports world didn't much mind what Judy did as long as she did not compete in thoroughbred contests where the big money was.

More than twenty years passed before women attempted to take the final step and become thoroughbred jockeys.

4

The Struggle

"If you let one woman ride in one race, we're all dead," a male jockey was quoted as saying in the late 1960s.

Many other jockeys shared the same feeling and sounded like prophets of doom. They gave a long list of reasons why women should stay in the kitchen and out of the saddle.

One reason was based on chivalry. The thinking behind it went like this: A man always helps a woman in trouble. On the track, the scene of many accidents and injuries, a male jockey would have to look out constantly for lady riders in trouble. This would disturb his concentration.

Another reason was based on the differences in physique. Since men have bigger arm and shoulder muscles than women, it was thought that girls wouldn't have the ability to control the reins of thundering 1000- to 1200-pound thoroughbreds as well as men.

Another reason was sheer nonsense. "I don't think their brains are capable of making fast decisions," wrote a famous male jockey.

Everyone who was against women riders competing in races conveniently forgot one thing: Women had already raced against men for decades, although not on any of the more than one hundred major thoroughbred tracks around the country. They had raced on what was called the "Leaky Roof Circuit": county fairs, carnivals, and minor tracks that were not governed by the rules and regulations of a state racing commission. In fact, as far back as 1932, Mrs. Lillian Jenkins Holder, a successful and experienced bush-league jockey, applied to a state racing commission for a jockey's license. This would have given her legal entrance to every big-time track in America, since a state jockey's license, like a state driver's license, is valid throughout the country. Mrs. Holder was turned down.

Circumstances were totally different in the 1960s. By then women were clamoring for their rights, and getting them. Important laws were being passed to help women in their drive for equality with men. The most significant was the Civil Rights Act of 1964. Title 7 of this bill made it illegal to discriminate in employment practices because of race, religion, national origin, or sex.

More than three years elapsed after the passage of this act before the first woman got not only the courage but also the legal and financial support needed to test the law at the track.

On November 22, 1967, Kathy Kusner applied to the Maryland State Racing Commission for a jockey's license. The petite, brown-eyed Kathy was twenty-seven years old at the time. She had been riding for the United States Equestrian Team for six years. She had competed in every major horse show in the world and had appeared in two Olympics. There was no question that she was brave and a master at handling horses. But did this mean Maryland officials would grant her a license? "No one wants to keep her from getting a license if she's qualified," a commission member said cautiously.

Kathy passed the first test every would-be jockey has to go through. She eased her mount into a starting enclosure, broke the horse out on a smooth, straight path when the gate swung open, and then raced for one-eighth of a mile in the company of other jockeys and their mounts.

The following day, the all-male commission denied Kathy a license. Their excuse? Kathy didn't want to get paid for being a jockey. She wanted to remain an amateur to compete in future horse shows and the next Olympics. A jockey must be a professional, the commission members publicly proclaimed. Nobody knows what they said in private.

Kathy reapplied for a license the following February. She was turned down for "lack of riding ability." She reapplied in April and again was rejected, this time because she supposedly lacked the strength to control a horse.

Armed with a woman lawyer and money from a foundation to aid women, Kathy went to court. She charged the commission with discriminating against her because she was a woman. The judge agreed with her.

Before making her racing debut, Kathy decided to enter the International Horse Show at Madison Square Garden in New York City. Misfortune struck. During the competition, Kathy's horse fell, rolled over on her, and broke her leg.

In the hospital Kathy was asked if she still planned to become a jockey when her leg healed. "I haven't changed my mind about anything," she replied.

Six days after the accident, Penny Ann Early was given the opportunity Kathy lost—the chance to become the first woman jockey to ride against men at a major track that allowed betting on the results of the race. The place was Churchill Downs, where the Kentucky Derby is held. Unfortunately it rained, and Penny Ann's horse was withdrawn from the field because it always ran poorly on muddy tracks.

A few days later, Penny Ann was scheduled to again ride at Churchill Downs. But the male jockeys threatened a boycott if Penny Ann competed, so she had to be replaced.

Next, Betty Jo Rubin, a nineteen-year-old with long pigtails, tried to be America's first woman jockey. A rock,

*A pony boy leads Penny Ann Early on Royal Fillet the day
she won the first horse race for women jockeys only—the
$10,000 Lady Godiva Handicap. (Suffolk Downs)*

Betty Jo Rubin brings home a winner in her first appearance at Aqueduct, New York, one of the most famous race tracks in the country. (Wide World Photos)

thrown by an unknown male rider, crashed through the trailer she used as a dressing room at Tropical Park in Florida. Male jockeys threatened to stage a walkout if they had to compete against a woman, and again the threat worked. Betty Jo was taken off her mount.

Penny Ann Early continued to try to break the sex barrier, this time at Santa Anita race track in California. Once again, the jockeys protested. Once again, Penny Ann was unable to race.

The girls' frustrations rose higher and higher as they kept pressing for their rights without any success. Yet despite all the obstacles, they knew that some woman jockey, somewhere in America, would finally clear the way for them. And they were right.

On February 7, 1969, Diane Crump rode in the seventh race at Hialeah, in Florida. Her mount, Bridle 'n Bit, started out strong but then faded back in the pack and finished tenth in a twelve-horse race over the mile-and-one-eighth course. Diane lost the race, but she won a spot in sports history.

Because it was such an exciting event, Diane was understandably nervous. She forgot to take off her watch before the race started, and she forgot to take off her horse's saddle and weigh in after the race ended. She had to be reminded to do both chores.

"It felt good out there. I think I'll be all right from here on out," Diane said when it was all over. "I really think I can make it now."

There was no holding back the rest of the women jockeys after Diane's race. Despite predictions like, "They won't last, they'll freeze, they'll panic," the girls started riding everywhere. And winning, too. Betty Jo Rubin did it first on February 22. She took the ninth race at Charles Town, West Viriginia, on Cohesion. She followed with winners at Waterford Park in West Virginia, Pimlico in Baltimore, and Aqueduct in New York, where she got the "initiation" given every jockey after a first victory at the track—a pailful of water was thrown in her face.

Diane Crump, America's first professional woman jockey, is also the only girl ever to ride in the Kentucky Derby. Her horse Fathom finished fifteenth in the race in 1970. (Hialeah Park)

Meanwhile, Diane Crump rode Bridle 'n Bit to victory at Florida Downs. After more triumphs, she became the first woman to win a stakes race, a big-money contest with top horses. She did it in a thrilling come-from-behind finish in the Spring Fiesta Cup at the New Orleans Fair Ground. In fourth place on East Lime as the horses hit the home stretch, Diane began whipping her mount, switching her stick from hand to hand. East Lime responded with the heart of a true thoroughbred, overtook the pace setter, and won by a length.

By April, 1969, there were more than enough women jockeys for the first women-only horse race, the Lady Godiva Handicap, run at Suffolk Downs in Boston. Penny Ann Early was the victor.

And in May, Mrs. Lillian Jenkins Holder reapplied for the jockey's license she had been denied thirty-seven years before. This time she was turned down because of her age instead of her sex. Still Mrs. Holder kept battling. Finally, two years later, in 1971, the Illinois Racing Commission licensed the sixty-two-year-old woman to work as an exercise girl, a job Mrs. Holder kept for two years. It was the most sentimental off-track victory ever won by a woman rider.

5

Famous Women Jockeys

Women jockeys drew large crowds during the first few months they were racing. The "jockettes," as they were sometimes called, were new, exciting, and different. But soon the novelty wore off. Even Kathy Kusner's eventual debut produced just an average turnout at the track.

Whether the women liked it or not, they soon became "one of the guys." If they were going to be successful as jockeys, they would have to do it because of their ability and not just because they could sell more admission tickets. Only the most determined women stayed.

By the end of 1969, Penny Ann Early had unsuccessfully turned to night club singing, and Betty Jo Rubin, who had been injured, was unable to lose the weight she had gained during her layoff.

Diane Crump finished the year as the top female in the money department. She won $110,476 for her horses' owners. But the woman who won the most races—fifty-five in all—

Jockey Mary Bacon does not want her young daughter, who is crazy about horses, to follow in mother's footsteps. (Hialeah Park)

was Mary Bacon. (Mary rode in races that offered less prize money than the ones Diane raced in.)

Mary Bacon is by far the most controversial woman in thoroughbred racing today. She rode at Raceway Park, Toledo, Ohio, when she was seven months' pregnant and lost her son, who was born prematurely. She posed for *Playboy* magazine. She signed lucrative advertising and promotional contracts with two well-known companies, and then was dropped by both after she made a speech at a Ku Klux Klan gathering. She has been fined by racing officials for abusive language. Once Mary was kidnapped by a crazy stablehand, and on another occasion the man, now in prison, shot at her.

Mary was born in 1948 in Evanston, Illinois. Her love affair with horses started early. Her mother says that Mary was climbing on ponies when she was five years old. After graduating from high school, Mary taught riding at the exclusive Grosse Pointe Hunt Club outside Detroit. Then she went to England, where she earned a British Horse Society Certificate after studying subjects like veterinary medicine and stable management. When she returned to the States, Mary went back to Grosse Pointe, then began working as an exercise girl, the job she held when she got married.

After Mary became a jockey, she received a great deal of publicity and attention. She was pretty, and she was a good rider. Her bravery and spirit impressed sports writers so much, they gave her the Most Courageous Athlete of the Year Award in 1973, a prize that usually went to a man.

Mary was once injured at Ellis Park, in Owensboro, Kentucky, and she entered the hospital suffering from a broken collarbone, contusions of the lung, bruised ribs, a concussion, and internal bleeding. Her doctor called her condition "serious." Twelve days later Mary was riding again. On another occasion Mary was in a disastrous accident at Pitt Park, in Pennsylvania. Exactly two weeks later she was back in the saddle.

"The only thing that got me where I am today is determination," the spunky jockey said. "To me, winning is a living. They'll have to put me six feet under to get me to stop racing."

Tough as she is, Mary is still very conscious of the fact that she's a woman. "I like being a girl and try to look like it even when I'm riding in a race. I wear big earrings, use makeup, and make sure of my nail polish."

In 1970 Mary won more money than any other lady jockey—$107,323. But in the following year she was overtaken by Robyn Smith, who held the title of leading woman jockey, in terms of money won, for four years in a row.

Robyn was born in California in 1942. Although she says, "Horses have always been my first love," Robyn didn't get involved with thoroughbreds until she was in her mid-twenties. Then she talked a friend into letting her exercise his horses at Santa Anita. She neglected to tell him she had never done that kind of work before. Recounting her first day on the job, Robyn said, "The horses weren't scared, but, boy, I was!"

Fearful or not, Robyn kept coming back to Santa Anita every day to ride and to learn. "I lived sixty miles away and that meant getting up at three in the morning. I was going to bed at 4:30 in the afternoon, and not minding it one bit," she said. "I had no social life for two years."

Robyn had only one complaint about being an exercise rider. "One of the frustrations of just working horses in the morning is you feel you've taught them something and established communication with them only to see somebody else ride them in the afternoon."

When women first started riding as jockeys, Robyn joined them, but she did not do well. She won only two races in 1969 and another two in 1970. Her career was going nowhere when she decided on a daring plan. She would come to New York, which gets first-class horses and jockeys, and propel herself to fame by riding there. To establish herself in new and strange territory, Robyn went to the stables at Belmont Park to apply for work as an exercise girl.

Robyn Smith holds the record for the most money won by a woman jockey in a year—$634,055. (Hialeah Park)

"I would go around and ask to get on a horse, but everybody said 'no.' Frank Wright [a trainer] said 'no,' and the next day he saw me coming back and it was 'no' again. But on the third day he started to feel sorry for me, so he put me on a horse to breeze and he breezed well. I guess I was lucky," Robyn said.

The year before she came to New York, Robyn's winnings totaled $10,947. The next year, her first as champion woman jockey, they skyrocketed to $278,246. During the summer season, she broke the record for seven furlongs (seven-eighths of a mile) at the Saratoga race track in upstate New York, riding Beaukins to the finish line in a blazing 1 minute, 21 2/5 seconds. Robyn's amazing gamble paid off. In one racing season she went from an unknown to a famous sports personality.

Said Robyn, "I think horses run kindly for me, although I couldn't tell you why. Maybe it's my touch. And sometimes when I breeze a horse, I feel almost telepathic communication with him. I just have to think 'more speed,' it seems, and the horse will turn it on. It could be something I do unconsciously with my hands that triggers him."

Robyn's first two big wins in stakes races in New York City were on a horse named North Sea, owned by a rich and powerful man who befriended Robyn, Alfred G. Vanderbilt. On March 1, 1973, North Sea was entered in the Paumonok Handicap at Aqueduct. There were six horses in the race, and North Sea was the outsider. But despite long odds, Robyn guided the horse to a four-length victory. Thirty days later Robyn and North Sea also took the Westchester Handicap and came within 1/5 second of tying the record for the mile at Aqueduct. Robyn won because of creative thinking. She kept her horse outside because North Sea always ran too hard too early when he was close to the rail and would not have had enough stamina left for a strong finish. Robyn also suggested taking off North Sea's blinkers, which blocked his side vision, and this change also helped the horse to win.

Robyn shares a problem with many jockeys—keeping her weight down. Any extra weight jockeys add to their bodies, even one additional pound, can slow a horse down and turn a winner into a loser. Robyn's predicament is doubly troublesome. She is 5'7", extremely tall for a jockey, and she easily puts on weight if she does not watch her diet.

What are her meals like? "I eat two pounds of ground lean beef a day, plus three or four grapefruits—and ice cream," said the jockey, who usually weighs about 110 pounds. "I broil the meat and eat it for lunch and dinner. No breakfast except a grapefruit and sometimes a cup of coffee."

Robyn was overtaken as the top woman money winner of the year in 1975 by Denise Boudrot. Denise, who was born in 1952, was brought up in Burlington, Massachusetts. Her father, who worked as a production foreman in a factory, bought her a horse when she was twelve. "I spent every day I could riding him," she said. "Actually I made up my mind when I was a sophomore in high school that I wanted to be a jockey," the 4'11" girl continued. "At that time, my father said that would happen only over his dead body. I found out later my father wasn't really concerned about my becoming a jockey. His main concern was that I stayed in school and graduated."

Denise dutifully listened to her parents, got her diploma, and even worked as a supermarket checkout clerk for a while. Then she went to Lincoln Downs, in Pawtucket, Rhode Island. While galloping horses there, she impressed an owner/trainer, who took her to his farm and taught Denise all the ins and outs of being a jockey.

She made her racing debut in 1972 and completed the year with only two wins. But she wasn't discouraged, and she worked harder than ever the following year. At one point Denise was getting up before 5:00 A.M. to ride at New Hampshire's Rockingham Park. Then she would go to Narragansett Park in Rhode Island for night racing. Finally, she would arrive home exhausted but ready to repeat the whole cycle the next day.

Jockey Denise Boudrot rides only in New England. (Suffolk Downs)

Denise Boudrot admits she's fallen in love with some horses she has ridden. (Suffolk Downs)

Denise was rewarded for her efforts. She began to be noticed, especially after she rode Isthatit, a horse nobody expected to win. It paid $188.60 for a $2 bet. Reporters nicknamed Denise "Longshot Lady," and her career gathered steam. By 1974, she had already won enough to buy a thoroughbred farm in South Carolina.

Denise has had her share of injuries, as have all jockeys. She wrenched her back in 1973, broke a leg in 1974, had a slight concussion in 1976, and tore ligaments in her shoulder in 1977. Still, she keeps riding. "If you let yourself get scared, there's no sense in racing because you're already beat," she says.

Denise is noted for the fact that she holds back her mounts and saves their energy for the home stretch. She comments, "I like it when I can sit back early in a race and wait until the turn to let my horse start running. I think that's my strongest type of ride. I don't like pushing on my horses leaving the gate. I like to let them get to running on their own and ask them for speed. I really love it when my mount is passing other horses on the turn and through the stretch. It's a fantastic feeling."

Despite all her experience and thousands of rides, Denise admits she still sometimes falls in love with a horse. The jockey, who races only in New England, says she is very happy with her life. "I have money in the bank and I don't want for anything, and I get along well with other jockeys."

6

Other Women at the Track and Farm

There are a number of women who train thoroughbreds or own them or the tracks where they run.

Marjorie Everett is the biggest shareholder in the corporation that owns Hollywood Park, in Inglewood, California. (Race tracks are owned by corporations, just like baseball clubs and other teams in sports.)

Mrs. Everett's father was Ben Lindheimer, who made millions of dollars in real estate. Mr. Lindheimer enjoyed horse racing. As a sideline business venture, he began investing money in tracks and courses. Eventually he gained controlling interest in the company that ran Arlington Park (thoroughbred racing) and Washington Park (harness racing) in Illinois.

"I'd gone to the track with my father when I was five," Mrs. Everett recalled. "I went into racing at eighteen when I started to learn the business. First I manned the switchboard at the track."

Karen Taylor is a co-owner of the great Seattle Slew, winner of thoroughbred racing's Triple Crown in 1977. Stablehand Donald Carroll stands to Slew's left. Jean Cruguet, the French jockey who regularly rides the horse, stands next to Karen. (United Press International)

In 1949 when Mrs. Everett was in her late twenties, her father had a heart attack and she became his chief assistant. Eleven years later, when her father died, she inherited the stock he had in the organization that operated Arlington and Washington. At that time she was the only woman in the country to head not just one track, but two. She fought mobsters who tried to become suppliers of laundry, liquor, and meat to her tracks in order to get her dependent on them for their services. She fired employees on the slightest provocation. She worked day and night, and did everything possible to increase the revenue at her tracks.

She raised the prize money at major stakes races, which increased the quality of competing horses and riders. She modernized the facilities. She tried to increase attendance by holding races after dark, and failed only because thoroughbred night racing was declared illegal by unsympathetic law officials.

Mrs. Everett's tracks eventually became so profitable that they attracted the attention of the giant Gulf and Western Corporation, which bought Mrs. Everett's shares in her corporation for well over $20 million. Under the terms of the deal, Mrs. Everett was to continue managing the tracks, and she received a long-term contract.

But soon Mrs. Everett and the executives at Gulf and Western became unhappy with each other, and she turned to new horizons. She bought tens of thousands of shares in the firm that owns Hollywood Park and became a member of the board of directors. Today Hollywood Park boasts the highest average daily attendance of any race track in the country, proof of the amazing feats that one woman can accomplish in thoroughbred racing if she has enough power and talent.

Karen Taylor is the co-owner of Seattle Slew, the triple-crown winner of the 1977 Kentucky Derby, Preakness, and Belmont Stakes. The tremendous interest that everyone had in Seattle Slew made Karen an instant celebrity and changed her life completely.

Karen grew up in Yakima, Washington. She attended the University of Washington and majored in elementary education. After that, she worked as an airline stewardess for three years. And now she and her husband, Mickey, live in an inexpensive trailer in spite of the fact that they own a famous thoroughbred.

Karen and Mickey have had incredible luck ever since they bought their first thoroughbred in 1973. The horse won its first three stakes races. It also gave the Taylors a taste of what the future might have in store for them.

In 1974, Mickey bought a horse named Lexington Laugh for his wife. According to Karen, "I went crazy over the horse. I got too deeply involved. I'd sleep in front of his stall."

Then the horse broke a leg and the Taylors were advised to destroy the animal. Karen refused. "I knew he could never run again but I wanted him saved," she said. "I wanted to keep him in the backyard and be able to look out the window and see him." Finally, after an operation on Lexington Laugh, Karen saw it was hopeless and the horse was put down. "I promised myself I would never again get attached to a horse if we ever came up with another good one," Karen said. But that was before Seattle Slew.

Seattle Slew was spotted at an auction in Kentucky in July, 1975, and bought for Karen by a veterinarian for a bargain $17,500. "He said, 'I think we have something special in the colt,'" Karen related. "That's when our hopes began to rise—even before his first race. But we never dreamed it would turn into this."

After Seattle Slew was trained carefully, he entered his first race as a two-year-old in September 1976. Karen then performed a ritual she has done before every Seattle Slew appearance. She went to the betting window and bought five two-dollar win tickets on her horse to keep as souvenirs.

In his debut, Slew first led by half a length, then two lengths, then opened it up to five lengths as he won easily. In less than a month, Seattle Slew won two more races, the last being the rich Champagne Stakes at Belmont Park. Facing a strong field, Slew was the front runner all the way and romped to a nine-and-three-quarters-length victory, setting a new record for the Champagne.

There were more valuable races for two-year-olds in the next few months, but the Taylors resisted the temptation of fast money. Instead, they handed the horse back to their trainer in order to give Slew every chance to develop into a top three-year-old. (The most famous races in America, including the Kentucky Derby, are restricted to three-year-olds.)

Before Slew's first race in 1977, Karen went to a big testimonial dinner to pick up a prize for having had the top two-year-old the previous year. She and her husband looked around at all the other couples and saw that they were two of the youngest owners there. Many others had raced horses for ten, twenty, or thirty years and never purchased a champion like Seattle Slew. "Here we were getting an award after so little time," Karen said, realizing how truly fortunate she and her husband were. "We have been very spoiled," she later remarked.

Despite money and glory, Karen still does much of the work around the stables. She walks, waters, and feeds all her horses, except for Seattle Slew. "He's too strong for me, and besides he's too valuable for me to be handling him."

Karen concluded with a four-word summation of her experience with Seattle Slew. "It has been fantastic."

Rosemary "Pinkie" Henderson is a trainer who gave up her marriage for horses. She got into her profession by accident. She and her ex-husband, Doug, who were living in Florida, started buying thoroughbreds in 1973. They hired one trainer, then a second, then a third, but were unhappy with each one. Finally, Doug persuaded Pinkie to try training the horses herself. She got her trainer's license in 1975.

That same year Doug got his mother interested in thoroughbred racing as a tax shelter and business venture. Doug's mother decided to enter the sport and bought a total

*Trainer Rosemary "Pinkie" Henderson discovered she loved
horses more than her husband. She divorced him to devote
all her time to her work. (Santa Anita Park)*

of 30 horses. One of them was Proud Birdie, son of the 1967 Kentucky Derby winner, Proud Clarion.

Pinkie trained Proud Birdie and did such an outstanding job that the two-year-old horse won the Christmas Handicap at Calder Race Track. Pinkie, who stands 6'1" tall, became addicted to her successes and her new life.

The male trainers at Calder gave Pinkie much needed help and assistance. "I guess they didn't think I was such a threat," she said. "They knew I was serious, though, when I started showing up at the track at five every morning. What I learned in six months, it would have taken a man six years to learn."

After her education and victories in Florida, Pinkie moved to California because, as she said, "I wanted to be where the class is."

Proud Birdie was bought by Doug Henderson from his mother in June, 1977 and the new owner kept Pinkie as trainer of the horse, but only temporarily.

However, Proud Birdie, who ran at Santa Anita, did not do too well and was a disappointment to Pinkie. After his initial failures Pinkie said, "He just doesn't like this track. I can't train him any better and he's in excellent physical condition. I've had him checked by the vet at least eight times, from top to bottom and front to back. And I don't think it's a lack of heart, either. I think it might be fear. He slipped two or three times his first time out and I believe he's afraid of the footing."

In August, 1977, Proud Birdie was shipped East and given a new trainer—a man. In October, 1977, the horse won the $250,000 Marlboro Cup. Did the new trainer have any secrets about handling Proud Birdie? "I didn't train him too hard," was all he would say.

Becoming a trainer may have wrecked Pinkie Henderson's marriage, but it made Lucy Delgado's marriage even stronger. Lucy got her trainer's license in 1975 after her husband, Roberto, had been a jockey for 17 years.

Trainer-housewife-mother Lucy Delgado gets help running her home from her daughters and husband, Roberto, who is a jockey. (Suffolk Downs)

Lucy had stayed away from the track in order to raise her two daughters. But then curiosity got the better of her. With more spare time on her hands, she started to learn about racing, and she became addicted to thoroughbreds.

Talking about her husband, Lucy said, "Before, I could never understand why he was always so tired ... now I know!"

Working closely in the same business hasn't caused any friction between Roberto and Lucy. In fact, when asked about her marriage, Lucy said, "It's better because we have a common interest now."

How does Lucy feel about being a trainer? What is her reaction to the long hours, pressure, and hard work? "I love it," she said. "I have learned a great deal, and I'm still learning." Then, after her initial burst of enthusiasm, Lucy added, "I do worry a lot."

Lucy has a great deal of affection for the horses she trains, which is obvious from one of the stories she tells. She was forced to leave a horse she had been training when she went to Florida. "When I came back, his leg was broken," Lucy recalled. "The look in his eyes almost tore me apart. He couldn't understand why I had left him. I cried for days."

7

More Opportunities

Horse racing is a wide field that includes more than just thoroughbreds, including steeplechasers. Standardbreds (trotters and pacers), and quarter horses (usually crossbred with thoroughbreds) run for cash prizes, expanding the work opportunities available for girls who love horses. And it is just as easy to get a job with standardbreds as it is with thoroughbreds. Some claim it is even easier. Again, all a girl has to do is present herself to a prospective employer.

There are more than 46,000 trotters and pacers currently in action, and over 13,000 new horses are registered to perform each year. Most of the tracks and fair grounds that feature harness racing are located either east of the Mississippi or in California. However, standardbred farms, like those where thoroughbreds are bred, are scattered all over America.

Compared to working with thoroughbreds, working with standardbreds has both advantages and disadvantages. One big plus is that there is no such thing as a hot walker, exercise girl, or pony girl in harness racing. Every girl who starts out automatically becomes a groom her first day on the job. If she does well and impresses her boss, she will start

Janet Irvine became a harness racing driver over her father's objections. Now she drives many of his horses. (United States Trotting Association)

exercising horses as well as grooming them. Learners begin in a jog cart, which is heavier than the sulkies drivers sit in during harness races. They take their horses clockwise around a track, the direction opposite to that in which races are held.

As she progresses, a girl will be allowed to let her horses pace or trot in the "right" direction. She will also give them freer rein to move faster.

The unfortunate thing about harness racing is that many trainers and owners drive their own horses during contests, since drivers don't have to be as light as jockeys. This closes the door to many grooms who want to move up and take part in the action on the track. If a girl wants to eventually be a driver, it helps to have a friend or relative who has a horse.

Bea Farber, unquestionably the best woman harness-racing driver in the country, is married to a driver-trainer who has a farm in Brighton, Michigan. She was employed as a legal secretary but kept pestering her husband to let her drive for him. Finally, in 1970, she had her chance and did well. The following year Bea's husband broke his arm. As unfortunate as this was, it gave Bea much more of a chance to drive and to show how extremely good she was. She has been winning many races and money since then. On May 21, 1977, she set a new women's record by driving Quick Command a mile in 1:55 3/5.

Quarter horses are so named because they race at breath-taking speeds for lengths of about a quarter of a mile, and, of course, the majority of races are run at distances of 350, 400, or 440 yards.

Most quarter-horse farms and tracks are found in the Southwest. One of the best-known courses is Ruidoso Downs, in New Mexico, the site of the All-American Futurity, the richest event in horse racing. Prize money for the contest, for two-year-olds, keeps going up and up each year and now totals over a million dollars. The race is so short and the horses are so fast that about 4/10 of a second separates the best from the worst.

Bea Farber, America's top woman harness racer, credits part of her success with horses to "a woman's touch." (United States Trotting Association)

Horses run flat out (at full speed) in quarter-horse races, so strategy, moves, and stretch runs are virtually nonexistent. A jockey's main job is to position herself and her horse correctly at the start for a fast break and be able to switch sticks from hand to hand to whip the horse on during the race.

Even though anyone with riding expertise can be a quarter-horse jockey, few women get mounts. Diane Crump rode in the Kentucky Derby in 1970, but it may be a long time before America sees a woman in the All-American Futurity, perhaps because quarter-horse people are more conservative. Still, they don't mind employing girls as grooms and hot walkers.

With more than 16,000 quarter horses actively racing, there are plenty of jobs for girls as long as they know they might not be able to advance as far as they might with thoroughbreds.

Steeplechase racing is confined mostly to the East Coast and California, which has a few important events. Steeplechase farms are located almost exclusively in the East, in such states as Maryland, Virginia, and South Carolina. The races are always long. The minimum distance is 1¾ miles. The length of the world's most famous steeplechase race, the Grand National in England, is 4 miles, 856 yards.

In the summer, steeplechase races are run at thoroughbred parks. In the spring and fall, events are held at farms and parks.

Steeplechasers start racing when they are four or five years old. Only at that age have their legs developed to the point where they can stand the tremendous tension and pressure of jumping. This means that thoroughbred horses can switch to steeplechasing as they grow older. Some older horses run in both steeplechasing and thoroughbred flat racing contests.

Women are as commonly found in steeplechasing as they are in other forms of racing. The most outstanding female jockey in the sport is Josephine Ruhsam. On May 30, 1977, she won the National Steeplechase Handicap and became

Janet Irvine often competes against her brother in harness races—and beats him. (United States Trotting Association)

the first woman ever to win a steeplechase stakes race.

Girls who want to work with horses have countless opportunities available to them, for there are job openings all over the country. Employers are as willing to hire beginners as they are to put experienced women on their payrolls. However, employers rarely advertise for help. If a girl sincerely wishes to work with horses, she must take the initiative and go directly to a track or farm. Once hired, she will find herself enjoying a special feeling of pride and satisfaction, and she can look forward to each new day because she will be putting her heart and soul into her job. And she, like so many other girls, will be performing a labor of love.